D1264097

The Doubleday
First Guide to Wild Flowers

THE DOUBLEDAY FIRST GUIDE TO

Wild Flowers

by Millicent Selsam

illustrated by Barbara Wolff

DOUBLEDAY & COMPANY, INC. GARDEN CITY, NEW YORK

List of Wild Flowers in this Book

Library of Congress Catalog Card Number 64-10143. Copyright © 1964 by Millicent Selsam. All Rights Reserved. Printed in the United States of America. First Edition.

ACKNOWLEDGEMENT. The author and artist thank Mr. Phil Clark, former editor of *Horticulture*, at present on the staff of the New York Botanical Garden, for checking the text and illustrations in this book.

How to Begin   The next time you take a walk, look for wild flowers. You will find them almost everywhere, even if you live in the city. They grow in city lots, at the edge of sidewalks, on lawns, and in parks. Of course you will find them in your back yard or if you walk through woods or fields or along country roads. Some wild flowers grow just back of sandy beaches, and around ponds and lakes. There are wild flowers on mountains and deserts too. The important thing is to start to look for them.

The flowers in this book are grouped according to color because it is easiest for a beginner to find the name of a flower that way. The main flower colors are yellow to orange, pink to red, lavender to blue, and white. Those are the bands of color you will find on the outside edge of the pages. If the flower is yellow, look for a picture of it on the pages with the band of yellow to orange color. Sometimes, one kind of wild flower grows in many different colors. Where this happens the flower is pictured in its most usual shade with the other colors mentioned.

Under each color, the flowers are separated into field flowers—those you find in sunny open fields, meadows and roadsides, and woodland flowers—those you find in shady woods. This sign ✸ is on the pages with field flowers. This sign 🌲 is on the pages of woodland flowers.

Next to the description of each plant you can find the season the flowers are in full bloom.

The flowers in this book are called by their common names. In different parts of the country these names may be very different. One person may call a flower jewelweed and a person somewhere else may call the same flower touch-me-not. But each plant has a scientific name which is written in Latin and is the same all over the world. For this reason the scientific name is listed next to the common name of each plant on the last page of the book. You don't have to learn these but it will help if you find people disagreeing about the name of a flower.

The scientific name is in two parts, as, for example, Solidago graminifolia. The first part, Solidago, is the *genus* and tells that the plant is a goldenrod. The second part of the name, graminifolia, tells the *species* or particular kind of goldenrod you are talking about.

There are thousands of different kinds of wild flowers in the United States. This book will introduce you to only a few of the most common ones. Turn the pages often and you will soon be able to recognize the flowers when you see them on your walks. After that you may want to go on to more advanced guides that will help you to know more and more wild flowers.

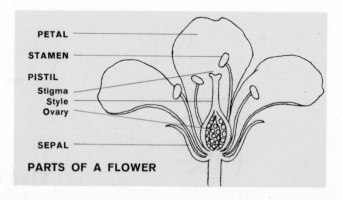

PETAL

STAMEN

PISTIL
Stigma
Style
Ovary

SEPAL

PARTS OF A FLOWER

SUMMER

Evening Primrose   This plant is tall and hairy with pointed leaves. There are four yellow petals on each flower. It is called evening primrose because the flowers open toward evening and close in the morning.

FALL

Goldenrod   There are more than 100 kinds of goldenrods in this country. Most goldenrods have big showy sprays of tiny golden flowers. Goldenrod does not cause hay fever. Another weed that blooms at the same time, ragweed, is the plant that makes people sneeze.

SUMMER

Dandelion   The dandelion is the best-known flower in the world. The "flowers" are really clusters of tiny flowers packed closely together. Take a flower head apart and see for yourself what each tiny flower is like. After blooming, the flower heads close up and a week later open into balls of gray fluff. Blow on this and each seed will take off into the air with its own silky parachute. The leaves can be used for salad.

Evening Primrose

Goldenrod

Dandelion

9

SPRING

California Poppy   This flower is the state flower of California. Hillsides along the Pacific coast turn gold when these cup-shaped flowers bloom in the spring.

SUMMER

Sunflower   Like the dandelion, a single "flower" is really a flower head made up of many little flowers. The outside flowers have yellow petals. The center flowers are usually brown and packed closely together. There are sixty different kinds of sunflowers. They get their name from the way the stems and flower buds turn from east to west following the sun.

SUMMER

Butter-and-Eggs   If you see a plant with yellow and orange two-lipped flowers, it is probably butter-and-eggs. You can tell why it is called this when you look at the colors of the flowers.

SUMMER

Buttercup   All buttercups have five buttery-yellow waxy petals. Look for them in meadows, and in and around marshes and ponds.

California Poppy

Sunflower

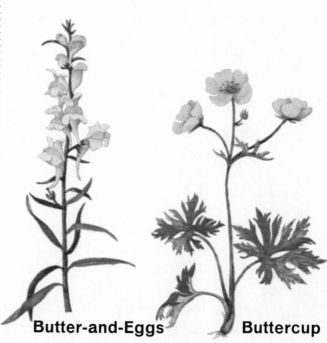

Butter-and-Eggs

Buttercup

11

Bellwort The large-flowered bellwort is one of several bellworts that grow in the east and into the midwest. If you take a walk through the woods and see a delicate plant with nodding bell-like flowers that droop under the leaves, it is likely to be a bell-wort.

Touch-me-not or Jewelweed This plant gets its touch-me-not name from the way the fruits spring open at a touch, scattering the seeds. The jewelweed name may come from the way the dew on the leaves glistens like jewels in the early morning. The flowers hang gracefully on slender nodding stems.

Trout Lily or Yellow Adder's Tongue In early spring some woods are carpeted with these plants. Notice the two mottled leaves at the base and the single nodding flower that looks like a tiny yellow lily. The trout lily name may come from the way the mottled leaves resemble the back of a brook trout.

Bellwort

Touch-me-not

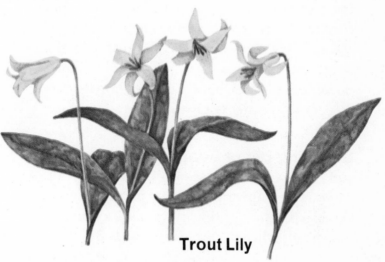

Trout Lily

SUMMER

Scarlet Painted Cup or Indian Paintbrush

You can find this wild flower throughout the prairies of the west. The leaves surrounding the flowers look as though they were dipped in a pot of red paint. There are 35 different kinds of painted cups. In some the leaves have a yellow stain instead of red.

SUMMER

Clover

The red clover is the most common field clover. Other clovers have white, yellow, pink or purple flowers. The tiny flowers are clustered together in egg-shaped heads. Take apart one of these heads and see what each flower looks like. Most clovers have leaves that are divided into three parts. Remember how hard it is to find a four-leaf clover?

SUMMER

Bouncing Bet or Soapwort

Along roadsides you are sure to find these pink flowers with notched petals. The soapwort name was given to this flower because the juice of the leaves is sticky and makes soapy suds when the leaves are crushed in water.

Scarlet Painted Cup

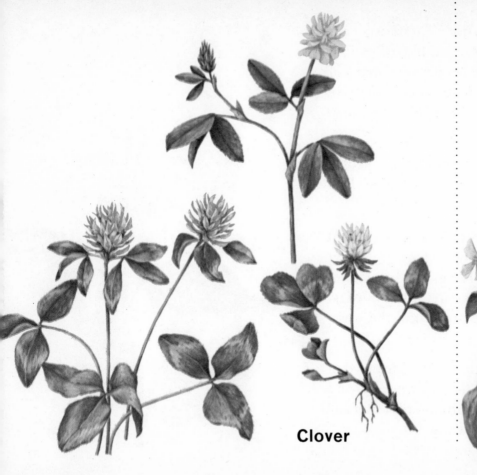

Clover

Bouncing Bet

15

Bee Balm or Oswego Tea   The flowers are clustered at the top and are shaped like tubes that open into an upper and lower lip. Some relatives of bee balm are pink or purple. If you think you have found this wild flower, feel the stem. It is four-sided.

Fireweed   After a forest fire, the first plant to spring up is the fireweed. The long pods open to show the seeds with their long silky hairs. This makes the plant look shaggy in the fall.

Shooting Star   Notice how the petals point backward and make the flowers seem to shoot forward. A cluster of oval leaves at the bottom surrounds the bare stalk that carries the flowers. Shooting stars are common in the central and western states.

Thistle   The common thistle is one of many that grow across the country. All thistles are spiny and prickly. The flower heads are often pink but some thistles are purple, yellow, or white.

16

Bee Balm

Fireweed

Shooting Star

Thistle

17

Spring Beauty This delicate pink flower blooms in the very early spring. On a bright sunny day the woodland floor turns pink with the open blossoms. This spring beauty grows in the eastern part of the country but it has close relatives that you can find in the woodlands of the west.

Wild Columbine Notice the long spurs on the nodding flowers. They sway on their delicate wiry stems when the wind blows. The leaves are divided into three parts and have scalloped edges. The red and yellow columbine grows in the east but there are blue, yellow, white and red columbines that grow in other parts of the country.

Red Trillium or Wake-Robin There are different kinds of trilliums, some white, some pink, some purple, but all have the parts arranged in threes. Look for three leaves and three petals. Trilliums are called wake-robins because the robins sing when they bloom.

Spring Beauty

Wild Columbine

Red Trillium

19

FALL

Gentian   Gentians are usually blue or purple and the petals are usually joined into a tube. Twenty different kinds of gentians grow over most of the country. The shapes of the flowers vary. Some have the shape of barrels or bottles, or vases. Some have smooth edges and others are fringed.

SUMMER

Milkweed   All milkweeds have leaves and stems that ooze a thick milky juice when cut. The flowers grow in clusters and may be pink, white or purple. When the pods open you can see the brown seeds with their silky white parachutes. Milkweed seeds can float through the air for many miles before coming to earth.

SPRING

Pasque Flower   While early spring flowers are blooming in the eastern woods, the western prairies turn purple with blossoms of the Pasque flower. After the flowers fade, you can see the seeds with their long silky tails that help them float through the air.

Gentian

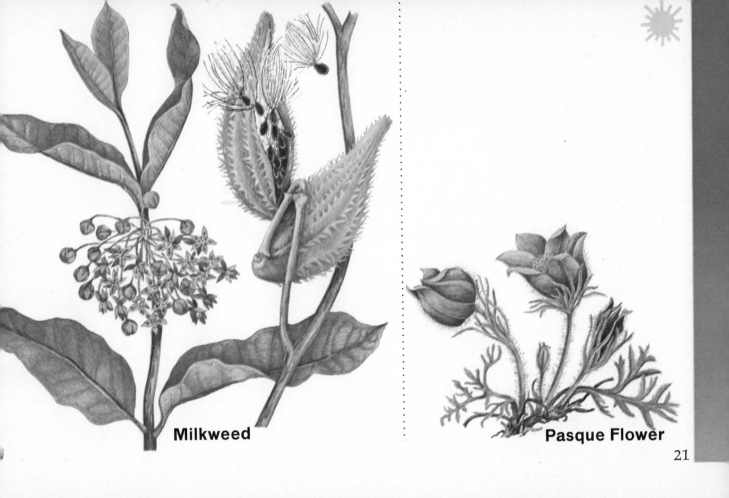

Milkweed

Pasque Flower

SUMMER

Chicory   This is a tall roadside plant with flowers that look like blue dandelions. The stems are sort of zigzag. The flowers open in the morning and close by noon. The roots are dried and ground to make the chicory that is often added to coffee mixtures.

SUMMER

Lupine   The wild lupine is one of 150 kinds of lupines. The flowers are clustered together in tall wands. Most lupines have leaves that are divided into parts that grow out from the center like the spokes of a wheel.

FALL

Aster   The name aster comes from the Latin word meaning star. The flowers really look more like purple daisies than stars. Asters add the purple color to fields of flowers in the fall. There are also pink, white, blue and yellow asters.

SUMMER

Bellflower   This is a delicate plant with bell-shaped flowers. Other bellflowers may be white as well as blue and purple.

Chicory

Lupine

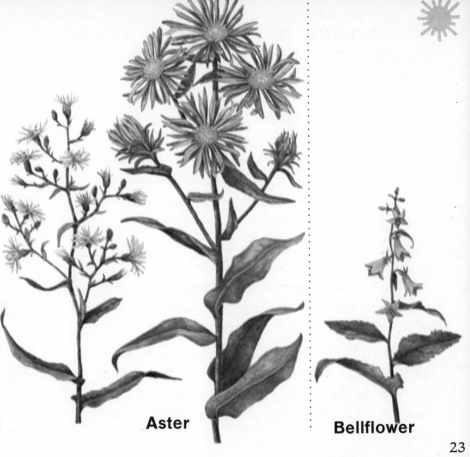

Aster

Bellflower

SPRING

Wild Geranium   The flowers have five petals. This plant is especially interesting because the seed capsule splits open, the parts coil up and toss the seeds out like a slingshot.

SPRING

Hepatica or Liverwort   This is one of the very first of the wild flowers to appear in the eastern woods in the spring. The pale blue to purple flowers are usually half hidden under decaying leaves and they are wonderful to find before the warm days of spring have really come.

SPRING

Wild Blue Phlox   The flowers are in loose flower clusters and are shaped like little trumpets. The petals are usually notched at the edges. This plant forms drifts of blue on the ground under the trees in most woodlands of the midwest.

SPRING

Violet   There are a hundred kinds of violets in this country. Besides the purple, there are blue, white and yellow violets. In the fall, notice the little boat-shaped parts of the fruits from which the seeds are shot out.

Wild Geranium

epatica

Wild Blue Phlox

Violet

25

SUMMER

Daisy You can find daisies in almost any field. The "flowers" are really flower heads with two kinds of tiny flowers packed together. The yellow flowers in the center are shaped like tiny tubes. Around them are the white "ray" flowers. When you pluck the daisy to find out if someone "loves you or loves you not," you are pulling separate flowers.

SUMMER

Queen Anne's Lace or Wild Carrot This is the wild plant from which our garden carrot was developed. The tiny white flowers are grouped in lacy, flat-topped clusters. The leaves are much divided and fern-like.

SUMMER

Mariposa Lily This flower looks like a small wild tulip. Mariposa lilies come in yellow and lilac as well as white. Notice how grass-like the leaves are. These lovely plants grow in meadows and foothills of the western mountains.

26

Daisy

Queen Anne's Lace

Mariposa Lily

SUMMER

Pearly Everlasting   The flowers are in flat-topped clusters. The flower gets its name from the straw-like flowers that last for a long time. The stems are woolly and white. This plant grows all across the northern half of the United States.

SUMMER

Bedstraw   These small delicate plants have weak stems that usually lean on other plants. They have the name bedstraw because they were once used to stuff mattresses. The rough bedstraw is one of 75 different kinds of bedstraws that grow in this country.

SUMMER

Boneset   This plant looks somewhat like a white goldenrod. But the stem seems to grow right through the leaves. A brew of the dried leaves was once used as a remedy for colds.

SUMMER

Yarrow   This plant has fern-like leaves and small white flowers in flat-topped clusters like the Queen Anne's lace. But there are many differences. Can you find them? Crush the leaves of this plant and smell the pungent odor.

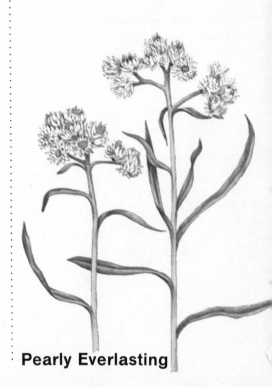

Pearly Everlasting

Bedstraw

Boneset

Yarrow

Bloodroot   Another beautiful flower found in the woods is bloodroot. Its petals are pure white. The name comes·from the red juice that oozes out from the underground stem when it is cut. Once the Indians used this juice to paint themselves and as a dye for cloth. After the flower dies the leaves grow rapidly and become very large.

Solomon's Seal   There are true and false Solomon's seals. True Solomon's seal has nodding bell-shaped flowers hanging along the stems. False Solomon's seal has tiny white flowers clustered at the top of the stem. The leaves of both look very much alike.

Dutchman's Breeches   The nodding flowers have two spurs that make them look like pairs of white breeches hanging upside down. The leaves are soft and resemble fern leaves. Look for this plant in the eastern woods.

30

Bloodroot

olomon's Seal

Dutchman's Breeches

31

Scientific Names of the Wild Flowers in This Book

Aster – *species of Aster*
Bedstraw, rough – *Galium asprellum*
Bee Balm (Oswego Tea) – *Monarda didyma*
Bellflower, common – *Campanula rapunculoides*
Bellwort, large-flowered – *Uvularia grandiflora*
Bloodroot – *Sanguinaria canadensis*
Boneset, common – *Eupatorium perfoliatum*
Bouncing Bet (Soapwort) – *Saponaria officinalis*
Butter-and-Eggs – *Linaria vulgaris*
Buttercup, common – *Ranunculus acris*
California Poppy – *Eschscholtzia californica*
Chicory – *Cichorium intybus*
Clover – *species of Trifolium*
Columbine, common wild – *Aquilegia canadensis*
Daisy, common – *Chrysanthemum leucanthemum*
Dandelion – *Taraxacum officinale*
Dutchman's Breeches – *Dicentra cucullaria*
Evening Primrose, common – *Oenothera biennis*
Fireweed – *Epilobium angustifolium*
Gentian – *species of Gentiana*
Geranium, common wild – *Geranium maculatum*
Goldenrod – *species of Solidago*
Hepatica, common – *Hepatica americana*
Lupine, common – *Lupinus perennis*

Mariposa Lily – *species of Calochortus*
Milkweed, common – *Asclepias syriaca*
Painted Cup, Scarlet – *Castilleja coccinea*
Pasque Flower – *Anemone patens*
Pearly Everlasting – *Anaphalis margaritacea*
Phlox, Wild Blue – *Phlox divaricata*
Queen Anne's Lace (Wild Carrot) – *Daucus carota*
Shooting Star – *Dodecatheon Meadia*
Solomon's Seal,
    True – *Polygonatum pubescens*
    False – *Smilacina stellata*
Spring Beauty, common – *Claytonia virginica*
Sunflower, common – *Helianthus annuus*
Thistle, common – *Cirsium vulgare*
Touch-me-not, Spotted – *Impatiens biflora*
Trillium, Red – *Trillium erectum*
Trout Lily (Yellow Adder's Tongue) –
    Erythronium americanum
Violet, common – *Viola papilionacea*
Yarrow, common – *Achillea millefolium*